RAIN FOREST BABIES

CROCODILE HATCHLINGS

by Genevieve Nilsen

I0793849

TABLE OF CONTENTS

tadpole books

WORDS TO KNOW

eggs

hatch

hatchlings

scales

tail

webbed

CROCODILE HATCHLINGS

What are in these eggs?

Baby crocodiles!

They hatch!

Each one is small.

It has a long tail.

Mom carries it.

Fun!

It has webbed feet.

It has scales.

It grows up!

It swims!

LET'S REVIEW!

Crocodiles are reptiles. Reptiles have scales. Point to the reptiles you see below. How do you know they are reptiles?

INDEX